D0598349

UNIVERSITY OF
TEXAS

CRESCENT BOOKS
NEW YORK

The publishers would like to thank Mr. Joe Roddy, Director of
Public Information at the University of Texas, for his invaluable
help in making available some of the photography shown in this
book, and for checking the accuracy of the text and captions.
Pictures of the Texas Longhorns pages 28-29 © 1986 Manny Rubio.

CLB 1535
© 1986 Colour Library Books Ltd., Guildford, Surrey, England.
Text filmsetting by Acesetters Ltd., Richmond, Surrey, England.
Printed and bound in Barcelona, Spain by Cronion, S.A.
All rights reserved.
1986 edition published by Crescent Books, distributed by Crown Publishers, Inc.
ISBN 0 517 61898 2
b w f e d c b a

"The Eyes of Texas are upon you
All the livelong day,"

And so begins the Texas alma mater. It all began in 1899, when university president William L. Prather ended a speech, "Students of the University of Texas, the eyes of Texas are upon you." This admonition became Prather's byword and the principle of the University.

In 1903, a student by the name of J.L. Sinclair set the maxim to song using the tune of "I've been working on the Railroad." Students, faculty and citizens loved it. From that day on, "The Eyes of Texas" was the official University song. In similar fashion other traditions were born at the University of Texas.

In 1884 a group of students from the four-year-old University of Texas traveled down to the train depot to see their baseball team off to a game with Southwestern University. The send-off looked pretty dull to some of the women. Where were the bright colors reminding them to bring a victory home?

Someone had a bright idea. They raced down to the nearest store and bought several bolts of ribbon in the only available colors – orange and white. And another tradition was born. In 1900 they made it official. Orange and white were the University colors.

Still later, in 1920 *The Alcalde*, the alumni newsletter, reported: "...in the scientific history of its development, the Longhorn comes to connote courage, fighting ability, nerve, lust of combat, efficiency in deadly encounters, and the holy spirit of never-say-die." If that description didn't reflect the fighting spirit of the University of Texas athletic teams, nothing did. So "Longhorn" was adopted as the official name of the teams.

The first official live longhorn mascot was presented to the student body in 1916 at the annual Thanksgiving Day game with Texas A&M. They called him Bevo. He worked his magic because the University of Texas won the day 21-7. The year before, it had been Texas A&M's victory at 13-0.

The students reported they would memorialize the day by branding Bevo with a large "T" and the "21-7" score. Protests of cruelty shelved this idea, but it planted the seed of a new one in the minds of the Aggies. Some three months later Bevo was seen sporting the very large numerals "13-0". What an embarrassment to a proud U.T. longhorn! Not to be outdone, the U.T. students devised a plan of their own. They cleverly changed the "13" to "B", the "-" to an "E" and inserted a "V" before the "0".

Bevo the First remained mascot for four years until he was served at barbecue January 20, 1920. He was followed in succession by twelve new Bevos, but none had the cachet or the bravery of Bevo the First.

The first campus football game was played on November 11, 1893. It was stopped after thirty minutes of play because the football had burst from being "too lovingly embraced." The first game with another school was that same year against Dallas. Texas won that one by 18-16.

By 1920 the University of Texas were champs. That year they had a 9-0 record, beating Texas A&M on Thanksgiving Day by 7-3. They were top of their conference and by 1931 they had captured two more Southwest Conference championships.

And then, in 1937, entered Dana Xenophon Bible, previously head coach at Texas A&M, where in eleven years he had won five Southwest Conference championships and then won six Big Six championships in eight seasons at Nebraska.

By 1941 Texas was ranked No. 1 in the nation and fourteen Texas players were featured on the cover of *Life Magazine*. But they then lost their next two games and finished number four in the final 1941 AP poll. As all good coaches go, so went Bible.

In 1956 the University of Texas was looking for a new coach again. They had heard about a 32-year-old out at the University of Washington. That's when they brought Darrell Royal in on a five-year contract. He stayed on at the University of Texas for almost 20 years, and during that time he brought the Longhorns to unprecedented heights. Thank you, Darrell Royal.

Football, baseball, basketball or academics, the University of Texas has grown from a small school in 1883 to a campus that today boasts an enrollment of 41,500 in Austin alone, and 13 satellite campuses. There are branches in Arlington, Dallas, El Paso, Odessa, San Antonio, Tyler and Medical or Health Centers at Dallas, Galveston, Houston, San Antonio and Tyler. Its a modern, down-home, yet sophisticated university system that does Texas proud.

Facing page: Texas Union, the University of Texas at Austin.

When it was established in 1883 the
University of Texas at Austin (these
pages and overleaf) occupied one
building on a 40-acre site. Today a
plethora of halls and houses, totaling
over 110 buildings, is located on the
University's main, 300-acre campus.
Right: Littlefield Fountain, which was
erected in 1932 as a memorial to those
students who served their country in
World War I. Far right: Littlefield
Fountain backed by the Main Building and
University of Texas Tower, the center of
the university's administration, (center
right) the modern Concert Hall, (bottom
right) Battle Hall, and (far right
bottom) the renovated 19th-century, Arno
Nowotny Building which serves as the new
visitor center. Overleaf: (left top) a
lawn between Mezes and Benedict Halls,
(left bottom) Goldsmith Hall, (right
top) the glass-walled Graduate School of
Business and (right bottom) a verandah
outside Texas Union.

Above: the vast Memorial Stadium, (top center) Texas Swimming Center, (top left) the Concert Hall, (left) looking towards the University Christian Church from Littlefield Fountain, and (far left) the Main Building and Tower, glimpsed (top) through the Burleson Bells. On occasions, the tower is lit bright orange in celebration of such events as sporting victories or special academic achievements.

Right: Greek and Roman sculptures and (top) modern design at the Huntington Art Gallery in the Harry Ransom Center, and (above) the Texas Union. Facing page: classes in (top) the Business Administration Building and (bottom) the Academic Center Auditorium.

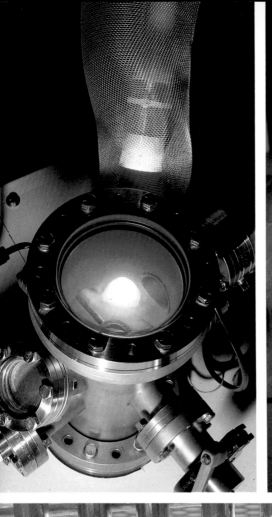

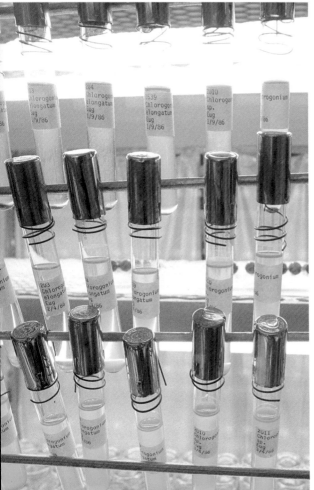
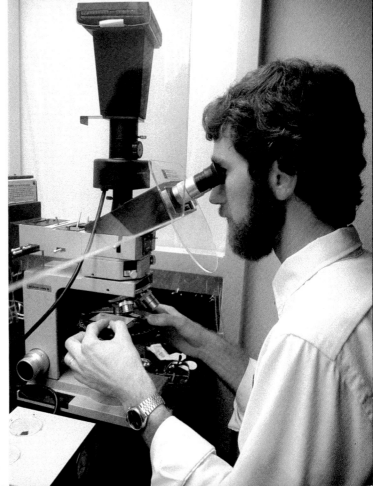

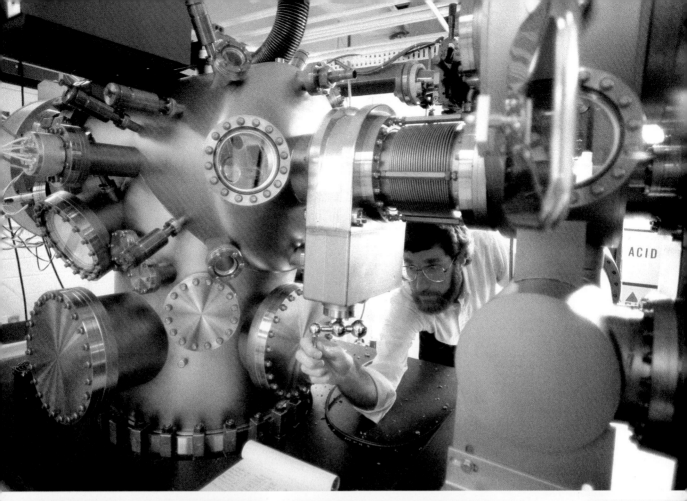

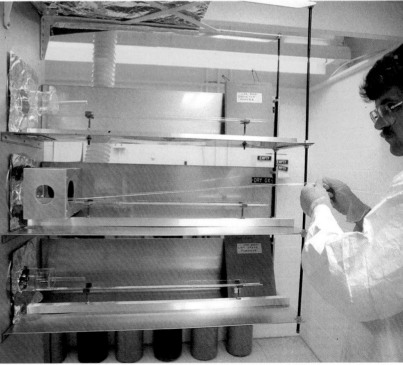

Since the 1984 launch of massive developments in its
science and engineering faculties, the University of Texas
at Austin has become a leader of reseach in these fields.
Left: experiments in the Physics Department, (facing page
bottom left) a culture collection of algae in the Botany
Department, and (remaining pictures) the Microelectronics
Research Center of the Department of Electrical and
Computer Engineering.

Top: the Lyndon Baines Johnson Presidential Library and Museum, (above) the Performing Arts Center, (right) University Avenue and the illuminated State Capitol seen from Littlefield Fountain, and (inset) the University of Texas Tower, Austin. Overleaf: (left top) Guadalupe St. or "The Drag", (left bottom pictures) the Texas Union, and (right) the Perry-Castaneda Library.

THE UNION
IT'S HIP,
IT'S HOT, IT'S HERE

In terms of sport, relaxation and welfare, the University of Texas at Austin has a wealth of amenities. Facing page: (top) an outdoor café and (bottom) student union, and (this page) the Frank Erwin Center, showing Texas beating Oklahoma at the NCAA Women's Midwest Regional Championship of 1986. Overleaf: (left top) Penick Allison Tennis Center, (left bottom) Perry Castaneda Library, and (right) students relaxing by Littlefield Fountain.

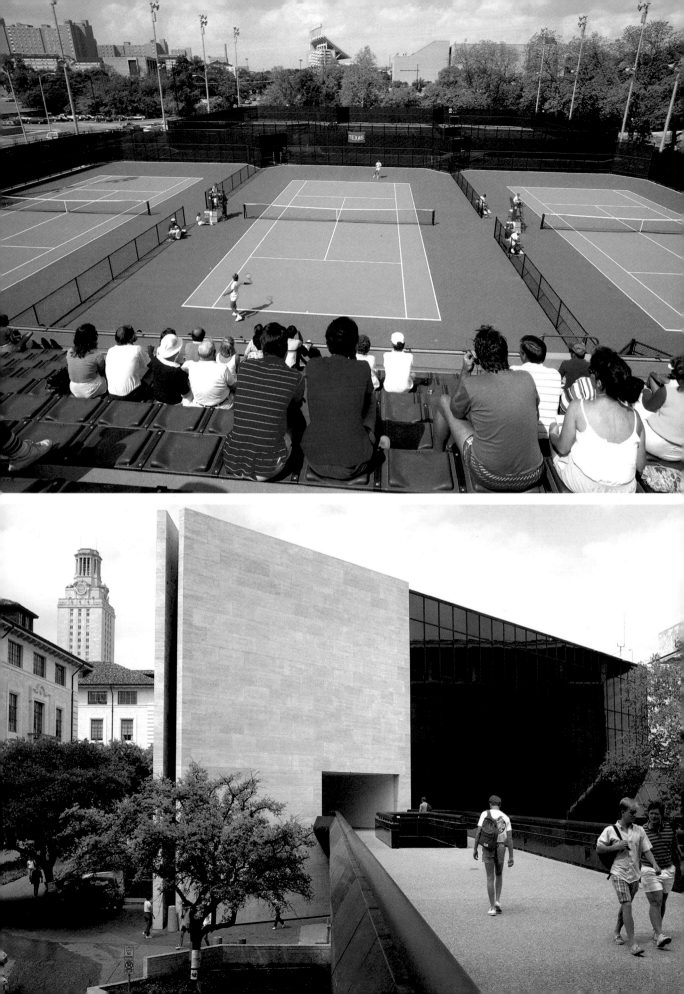

Top far left: a statue of George Washington, backed by the Main Building and University of Texas Tower, (far left) Littlefield House, and (remaining pictures) the Lyndon Baines Johnson Library and Museum. The library was established by Lyndon B. Johnson when he left the Presidency, and the museum contains various biographical displays, including a replica of the Oval Office (top and center left), and the Head of State Gifts (top center).

Facing page bottom: the 1985 Commencement ceremony. Right: gardens near the Computation Center and (bottom) along East Mall. The pleasant grounds of the University of Texas at Austin (remaining pictures) provide students with numerous opportunities for taking the weight off their feet.

Over 1,900 athletes competed in the Texas Relays of 1986 (these pages), which were held at the magnificent Memorial Stadium at Austin. As well as various relay races, this exciting event involves games ranging from discus throwing to pole vaulting and is now recognised as one of the best athletics meetings of the year. Overleaf pages: Texas Longhorns in action on the football pitch.

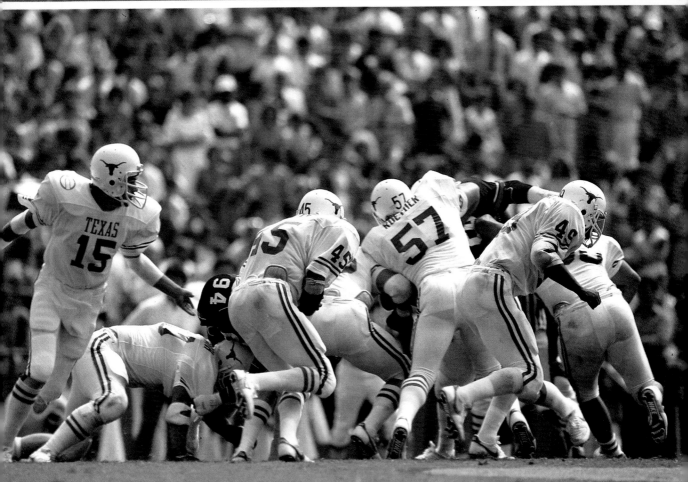

Left: for man and beast alike, the university's attractive grounds provide tranquil seclusion from the bustle of Texas' capital city. Flower beds line East Mall (facing page) and border many of the fine buildings on campus. Students wearing mortarboards and gowns trimmed with the University of Texas orange make a fine spectacle at the 1984 Commencement (above).

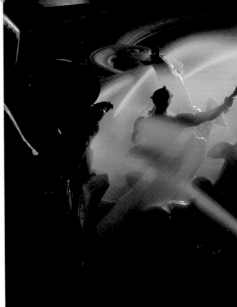

Above: the University of Texas Tower, (right) the Texas Swimming Center, (above right) Lyndon Baines Johnson Presidential Library and Museum, (top right) Littlefield Fountain at night, (far right) the Concert Hall, (center far right) the Garrison and (top far right) the celebrated Texas Longhorn, the mascot of the University of Texas at Austin.

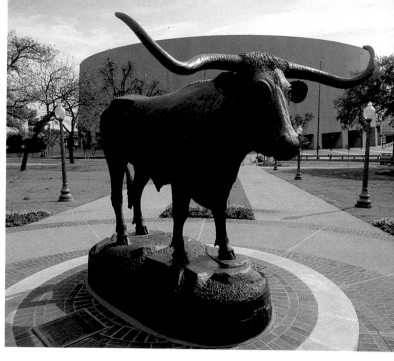

The University of Texas at Dallas
(these pages), which was established in
1969, is located on a 600-acre campus
with fine modern buildings and
facilities covering over a million
square feet. Above: sculpture outside
the University of Texas Health Science
Center at Dallas, and (below) the Cecil
H. Green Center.

Top: the Eugene McDermot Library, (facing page top) the Union and (remaining pictures) the University of Texas Health Science Center at Dallas, which was established in 1972 and deals with many important aspects of health education, research and patient care.

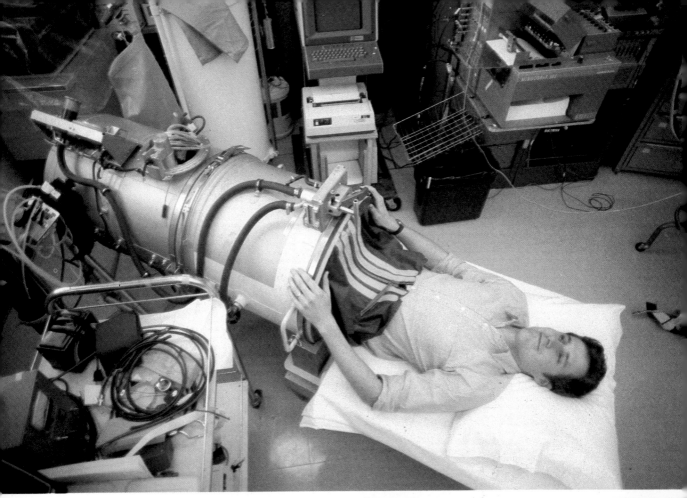

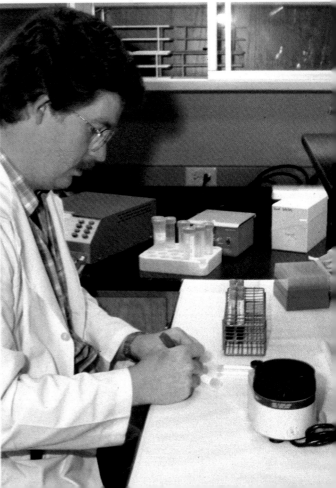

These pages: work in progress at the University of Texas Health Science Center at Dallas, showing the Human Nutrition Center (right) and, at the Space Medical Lab., experiments with a lower body negative pressure device (top) and respiration and cardiac activity monitors (facing page).

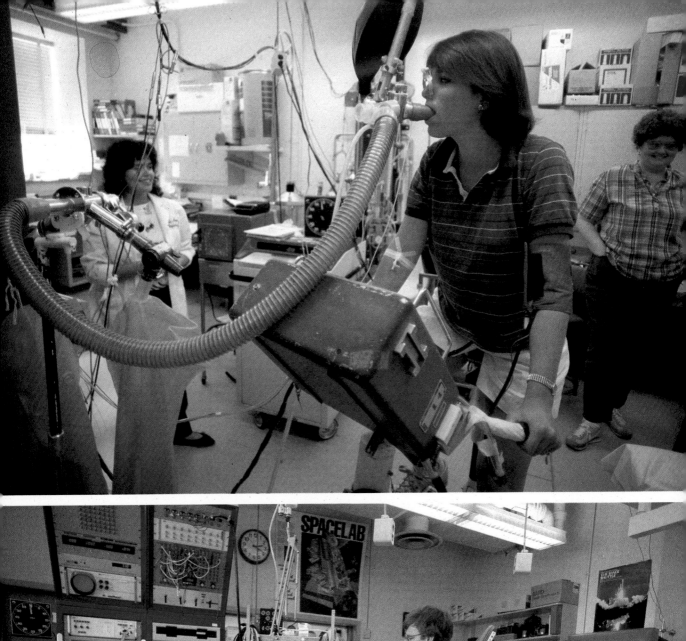

In a tranquil setting of reflecting pools, fountains and small trees, the Cecil H. Green Center (these pages) typifies the kind of cool and sophisticated modern architecture that makes the Dallas campus so restful to the eye.

The University of Texas at Arlington (these pages and overleaf), located between Dallas and Fort Worth, has an attractive, 340-acre campus characterized by red-brick buildings of innovative design. At present it enjoys the second largest enrollment in the University of Texas System, which it joined it 1965. This page: modern sculpture and libraries, (facing page top) Texas Hall and (facing page bottom) the School of Nursing.

These pages: aerial views of the Texas Medical Center, two miles south of downtown Houston. Within and around this vast complex of hospitals and institutions are units of the University of Texas Health Science Center at Houston, which provides a broad range of services including research, biomedical education and treatment.

The University of Texas at El Paso (these pages) occupies distinctive,
Bhutanese-style buildings in a fine campus overlooked by the Franklin
Mountains. Above: the Sun Bowl Stadium, (top) the Union and (remaining
pictures) the library. Overleaf: the University of Texas at Austin, with
(left top) the 1984 Commencement, (left bottom) the Computor Science
Lab., (right top) a Language Lab., and (right bottom) a zoology student.

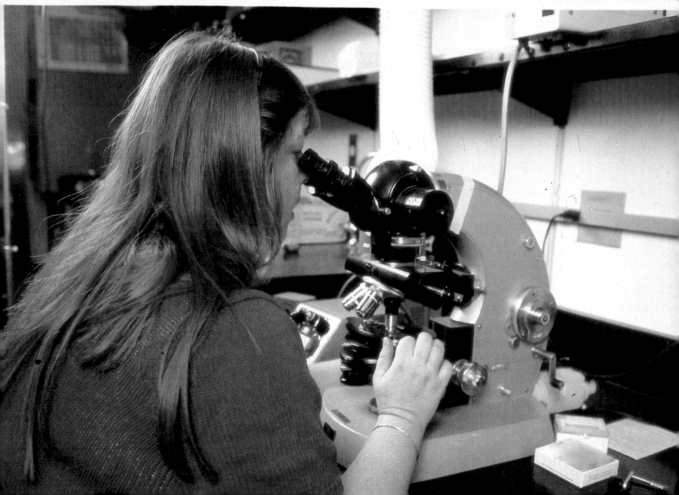

These pages: the University of
Texas at Austin, showing (top)
the Burleson Bells, (above)
the University of Texas Tower,
and (facing page bottom) the
1984 Longhorn Band. Off campus
are (left) the McDonald
Observatory in West Texas and
(facing page top) the Marine
Science Institute at Port
Aransas, with its attractive
boat the *Longhorn*.

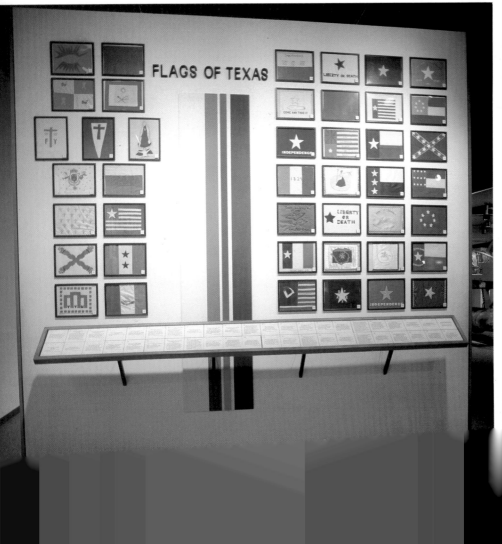

FLAGS OF TEXAS

Previous pages: The University of Texas at Austin, with (right top) Statues of the Muses at the Centennial Park, (right bottom) an aerial view of the campus from the south, and (left) the Mustang Statue. Also part of University of Texas at Austin is the McDonald Observatory (top left) at Mount Locke in the Davis Mountains. Far left: Flags of Texas and (left) Anglo-American exhibits in the University of Texas Institute of Texan Cultures at San Antonio, and (remaining pictures) the University of Texas Health Science Center at San Antonio, which is set within the 683-acre South Texas Medical Center.

Left: the library and (above left)
medical students attending a lecture at
the University of Texas Health Science
Center at San Antonio (top). Remaining
pictures: the remarkable, 600-acre
campus of the University of Texas at San
Antonio, where the academic programme
has been constructed around the needs of
those in the South Texas area.

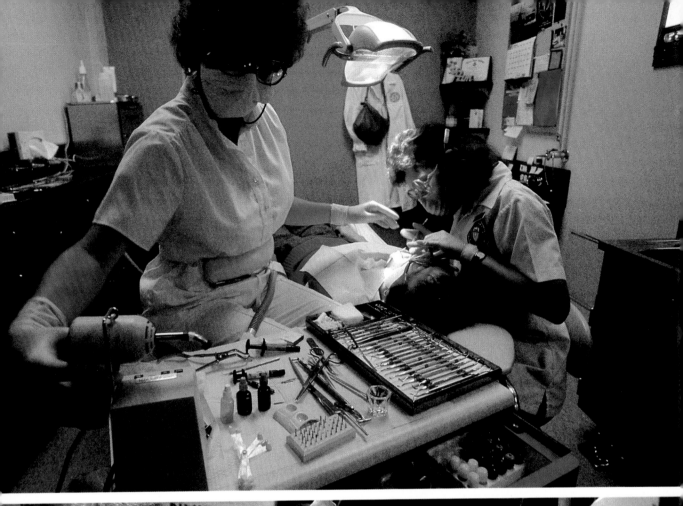

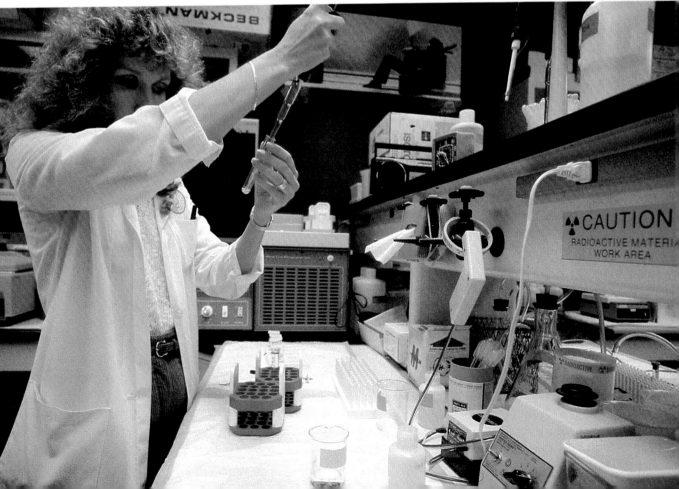

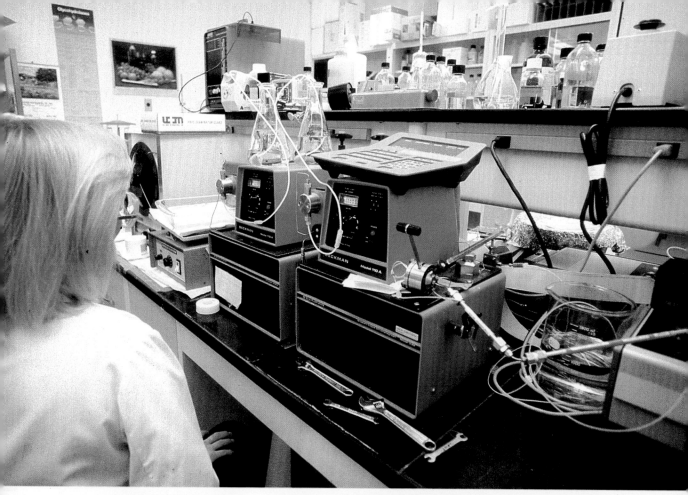

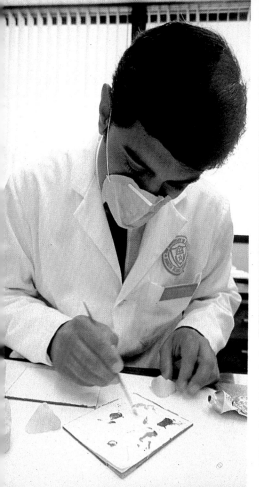

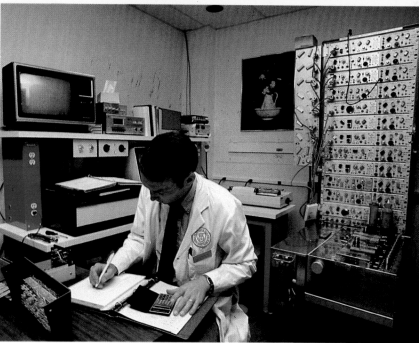

These pages and overleaf: scenes from the University of Texas Health Science Center at San Antonio, showing (left) artificial face parts being made at the Maxillo Prosthetics Clinic for those who have been disfigured by cancer, birth defects or accidents, (above) biofeedback and sleep research at the Behavioral Medicine Lab., (facing page top) dental students simulating a private practice, and (remaining pictures) blood research. Final page: the floodlit University of Texas Tower at Austin.